IMAGES
of England

CHALFONT
ST GILES

Souvenir of Milton's Cottage.

MILTON

Chalfont St Giles' only claim to fame is as the one-time home of John Milton, and this 1910 card features both the exterior and the interior of his cottage.

IMAGES
of England

CHALFONT
ST GILES

Compiled by
Colin Seabright

TEMPUS

First published 2002
Copyright © Colin Seabright, 2002

Tempus Publishing Limited
The Mill, Brimscombe Port,
Stroud, Gloucestershire, GL5 2QG

ISBN 0 7524 2463 7

Typesetting and origination by
Tempus Publishing Limited
Printed in Great Britain by
Midway Colour Print, Wiltshire

Multi-view postcards have always been popular, giving several pictures for the price of one. This 1910 card includes seven of the most popular views of the village.

Contents

Acknowledgements   6

Introduction   7

1. The Northern Hills   9

2. Valley of the Misbourne   25

3. The Village Pond   35

4. The Village Green   41

5. St Giles Church   53

6. High Street   59

7. Dean Way   77

8. Three Households   91

9. Old Jordans   95

10. Jordans Village   109

11. Seer Green   121

Acknowledgements

All the pictures are taken from postcards, books and photographs in my own collection.

I express my sincere thanks to the original photographers, mostly anonymous, and the publishers who made their work more widely available, and also thank those, both visitors and residents, who bought the postcards and sent them to their friends, who, in turn, saved them for many years in their own collections.

I also acknowledge my gratitude to the authors of guidebooks, whose works have been quoted or consulted for historical detail.

All the earlier pictures are now out of copyright, but the position is unclear with regard to the more recent illustrations, and I apologize here to any copyright owners who have not been consulted.

Dating from 1928, this drawing of the centre of Chalfont St Giles, including the pond, the green and the church, admirably captures the serene atmosphere of the village.

Introduction

Prehistoric flint implements and ancient British and Roman coins have all been found at Chalfont St Giles, and it is now known that a Roman highway linking their cities of St Albans and Silchester crossed the Misbourne and passed through the site of the village.

The derivation of the place name Chalfont has been a matter of debate for over a century. The second syllable means fountain or spring, but the origin of the first could be either *Ceadel*, a personal name, *cealc*, chalk, or even *chald*, cold. Whatever the origin, Chalfont St Giles is first recorded separately from St Peter in the middle of the thirteenth century, when the medieval manor lay within the hundred of Burnham, one of the Chiltern Hundreds, the stewardship of which, as a nominal position of profit under the Crown, still provides an escape route for a Member of Parliament wishing to relinquish his seat.

The 'Chalfont Country' in the Misbourne valley, situated between the old Oxford and Birmingham roads, was bypassed by main traffic routes and isolated from the busy world. Being in the vast Diocese of Lincoln, the area felt even more isolated from its seat of religious authority, and experienced a weakening of the hold of the official Church, becoming 'the very focus of Lollard and Puritan feeling' and a stronghold of the Quaker faith.

Major national events also bypassed Chalfont St Giles, but many of the principal participants had local connections or even lived there, the most important at The Vache. The history of that estate is far too complex to record here, but among its many residents over the centuries it numbers the Fleetwood family, which included the Treasurer of the Mint, a member who signed the death-warrant of King Charles I, and another who married a daughter of Oliver Cromwell.

The Cromwells had other connections with this part of Buckinghamshire and Oliver slept at The Stone after the battle of Aylesbury in 1642, when his troops were camped in The Stone meadows. While there, the troops used the church for unofficial target practice, taking pot-shots at the windows. This was confirmed by the craftsmen restoring the church fabric in 1861, who found small iron cannon-balls embedded in the stonework of the east window.

In 1665, the poet John Milton wanted to escape from the plague in London, and his friend, the Quaker Thomas Ellwood, arranged for him to rent a recently built cottage at the top of the High Street. Many of his closest friends were of the Quaker faith, worshipping in members' homes and farmhouses, and suffered dreadful persecution from magistrates including the local squire, because any form of worship other than at the Established Church was then illegal. Jordans Meeting House was built by the Quakers in 1688, immediately after the Toleration Act legalized their gatherings.

Chalfont St Giles remained a quiet village in the remote Misbourne valley, unknown except as the one-time home of Milton and as a centre for Quakers, avoided by main roads and railways until the end of the nineteenth century, when the arrival of the Metropolitan Railway at Chalfont Road, some 3 miles away, brought the Chalfont Country within comparatively easy reach of London.

Writing in 1896, the Rector of Chalfont St Giles records that 'Travellers to Chalfont St Giles have reason to bless the Metropolitan Railway. Until this railway was made it was singularly difficult to reach the Chalfont District. The London and North Western Railway on one side, and the Great Western on the other, have long familiarized the public with the towns and villages they have brought to light or created, but the long district from Uxbridge to Chalfont, Amersham, and Missenden has remained comparatively unknown and little visited. Even the coaches which used to run along this road to Wendover and Aylesbury were gradually starved and extinguished by the railways, and the result has been that an atmosphere of seclusion and of the past has settled down upon the Chalfont Valley, which makes it hard to realize that it is little more than 20 miles from Marble Arch. The extension of the Metropolitan

Railway to Aylesbury has at last penetrated these Buckinghamshire wilds, and soon after leaving Rickmansworth the traveller observes, by the change of scenery, that he is entering a very different country from that which he usually associates with the neighbourhood of London. He finds he is in a land of hills and valleys, a country in which thick beech-woods alternate with stony fields upon the bleak uplands, and soft meadows stretch along the plain.'

In a 1904 guide, the Chalfont Country is described as marked by the quiet undulations of the chalk country with soft slopes of grey grass or red-brown corn, falling gently to dry bottoms, with woodland flung here and there in masses over the hills. The predominant tree was beech, known as the Bucks weed, raw material for the local industry of chair-making, which was carried on in the parish, though not to such an extent as in the Wycombe area. Chalfont St Giles was also noted for its cherry-trees, of which a local variety attained an exceptional size, and for the sight of the spring blossom in the cherry orchards, particularly in the southern half of the parish around Three Households and Seer Green.

Even with the Metropolitan Railway, the nearest station is Chalfont Road, now called Chalfont and Latimer, just outside the extreme boundary of the parish, which includes a considerable tract of upland country north of the Misbourne valley. Although the later Great Central line crosses the valley near Chalfont St Peter, with a halt at Seer Green, neither can be said to serve Chalfont St Giles, which therefore remained comparatively isolated until the coming of the motor car, and has still avoided the worst development associated with London's commuter belt.

Again in 1929, a book on the 'Penn Country', which included the Chalfonts, refers to the area as 'still a sanctuary, a place of quiet beauty, not far from London, where those who love such things can find a patch of genuine country England' and this was despite a doubling of the population in the first twenty years of the century. It also appreciates that most of the building had been concentrated in well-sited groups with minimal effect on the district at large, but deplored ribbon development and the isolated settlements spread about the country, where a single garish villa could spoil a whole valley.

Later still, a writer in the early fifties confessed that until he set out to gather material about the area for his book he knew very little of this corner of England, but having visited it, he realised what he had missed, and planned to return many times to 'one of the most delightful districts he had ever visited'.

Now, another fifty years on, some commuter development has taken place, but has been kept back from the village street, which still retains its peaceful old-world character with mainly small, family-run shops, rather than faceless multiples. Even the traffic is still fairly quiet in the High Street as it leads nowhere in particular, and most motorists speed along the main road past The Pheasant, oblivious to the charm of the village they have avoided.

Throughout the first half of the twentieth century, virtually every ramblers' handbook or guide to Buckinghamshire chose the Metropolitan line as the approach to Chalfont St Giles, then followed Nightingales Lane past Pollards Wood and The Vache estate, arriving at the village via the Pheasant Inn. They then passed the pond and green, continuing up the High Street and past Milton's Cottage to Jordans, then within Chalfont St Giles parish, but recently combined with its neighbour to form the new parish of Seer Green and Jordans. For want of any better plan, the pictures in this volume are arranged roughly in a geographical sequence following that route, with the occasional detour to places of interest just off the main path, and ending at Seer Green.

Accurate dating of postcards is extremely difficult even for used cards, where the only certainty is that the publication date was before the postmark date. Therefore the dates given for most of the illustrations must be taken as informed estimates, probably accurate to within five years.

One

The Northern Hills

Standing at the crossroads on the Amersham Road, The Pheasant Inn has always been the accepted gateway to the village of Chalfont St Giles, the centre of which lies in the valley behind the inn. Hardly recognizable as the pub we know today, the sixteenth-century Pheasant is pictured in around 1880, still revealing its original brickwork. At this date the Wendover to London stagecoach still called here every morning at 8.30, returning in the early evening. After the opening of the Metropolitan Railway, Thomas Williams, a coach proprietor in the village, ran a 'conveyance' to Chalfont Road station in connection with certain fast trains to and from London. Chalfont St Giles Parish extends almost to that station, and this chapter features places of interest on the high ground from there to the start of the village at The Pheasant.

This is the way most visitors to Chalfont St Giles arrived in around 1900. The train from London is just pulling in to Chalfont Road station. The station was situated in the middle of

nowhere, a quarter of a mile from the junction of the main Rickmansworth to Amersham Road
and the lane to the Chalfonts.

On a very wet afternoon in September 1933, the 3.25 from Marylebone stands in the station which had been re-named Chalfont & Latimer in 1915. Some of the embryonic Little Chalfont village can be seen over the railway wasteland.

In the mid-thirties, this was the extent of Little Chalfont village, seen from the newly constructed Station Approach. The first few shops, the Sugar Loaves pub, a garage and the telephone exchange face the 'Donkey Field' across the main road. In the distance the first shops of Nightingales Corner stand by the turning to Chalfont St Giles.

Turning at Nightingales Corner into Cokes Lane, the first significant feature in Chalfont St Giles parish was Harewood Downs Golf Course. Opened in 1907 as a very exclusive club, this rather faded photograph of a group of players was taken about fifteen years later.

18 HOLES, LENGTH 5448 YARDS

SSS 69

Secretary:	R. N. Fowler
Professional:	Geoff Morris

Telephone:

Secretary:	Lt. Chalfont 2418
Professional:	Lt. Chalfont 4102
Clubhouse:	Lt. Chalfont 2308

VISITORS FEES:
ON APPLICATION TO THE SECRETARY

In the mid-sixties the club was advertising for members to play on its beautiful course, laid out over the former fields of Harewood Downs Farm. All of this was once part of the vast Vache Estate, extending down the side of the Misbourne valley to the main Amersham Road, where the original Harewood Downs House still stands.

In the first decade of the twentieth century parts of Pollards Wood, within the Vache Estate, were sold off for the development of large country houses, designed by eminent architects of the day. Pictured around 1920, this one, known simply as Pollards Wood, was built in 1907 and is now owned by a research company, which grafted a modern block of laboratories onto the house in the eighties.

Also built in 1907 within Pollards Wood, Pollards Wood Grange was designed by James Edwin Forbes in the style of a large cottage. It is shielded from the road by this thatched gatehouse, pictured within a few years of construction.

A little further along the way to Chalfont St Giles, Shortenills stands in another wood on the other side of the road, which also once belonged to the Vache Estate. Occupied from the late twenties by a Captain Hogg, he opened a preparatory school there in the thirties, when this postcard was published. More recently the estate grounds have been used as a Rural Studies Centre.

We now come to the remaining part of the Vache Estate, reduced to a mere 86 acres of parkland from the original vast area, which at one time extended the best part of 2 miles in both directions. This 1918 view from the north front of the house includes the Cook monument in the adjacent field.

The extent of the formal garden, close to the south-east corner of the house, c. 1900. The remainder of the estate was then reserved for the rearing of pheasants, who, during their short lives, were given the freedom of the lawns around the house.

This view of the east front of the house, reflected in the sizeable lake below the lawn, was taken shortly after the National Coal Board bought the estate in 1955 for use as a Staff College. They made considerable alterations, including the demolition of the old stable block, replacing it by a new wing to accommodate the students.

In 1777 The Vache was purchased by Admiral Sir Hugh Palliser, a close friend and admirer of Captain James Cook, who discovered Australia. The Admiral erected this monument to Captain Cook's memory in 1779. Pictured in the thirties, it consists of a globe, mounted on a square plinth with a long eulogy to the 'renowned navigator'.

CAPTAIN COOK'S MONUMENT, CHALFONT ST. GILES.

Vache Drive, c. 1900. During the Second World War American soldiers occupied Nissen huts erected on both sides of the drive, and in 1946, after the Yanks' departure, the encampment was taken over by some 200 homeless people in the country's first mass squat. They stayed for several years until sufficient council houses were available.

Opposite the entrance to The Vache, Gorelands Lane leads past the creeper-clad farmhouse from which it takes its name, set back among open fields. This card was produced around 1898, before messages were permitted on the address side (then officially the front) of postcards, so a space was left for brief greetings on the picture side.

This card shows the garden front of Newlands Park in 1914, when it was used as a sanctuary for suffragettes, and was sent by a newly appointed member of the household staff to his mother, reporting how happy he was. With adjacent modern additions, Newlands Park is now a campus of the Buckinghamshire College, and the extensive grounds include The Chilterns Open Air Museum.

A side turning leads to the Chalfont Centre of the National Society for Epilepsy, pictured here in around 1920 from the top of their water tower. Originally known as The Colony, the several gabled country houses, the first of which dates from 1895, were laid out in a wooded rural setting on the fields of Skipping Farm where the earliest residents found employment.

Pictured around 1920, The Nook and Sunnyside were the two big houses on the main road, respectively on the left and right of Vache Lane opposite The Pheasant. Sunnyside, with a footpath alongside, had been the home of a butcher who carried out his trade from a large hut in his garden until he moved to the Crown in the High Street.

Posted in 1906, this card shows the magnificent line of elm trees, the continuation of an avenue through the grounds of The Stone, which lined the main Uxbridge to Amersham road as far as Mill Lane, the back entrance to Chalfont St Giles.

The Pheasant pictured around 1900 after the brewers, Wellers of Amersham, had covered the ancient brickwork with rendering and mock timbers in the popular Brewers' Tudor style, and added a new section to the left hand end, slightly taller than the original. Advertising 'Horses & Traps to let on hire', they had also provided a drinking trough at the roadside for resident and visiting animals.

A companion to the previous card, this shows the Tea Garden behind The Pheasant where patrons could relax with refreshment and beautiful views over the village across the greensward of Stone Meadow.

Among the visitors to Chalfont St Giles in the early years of the twentieth century were parties of Londoners on their company outings. This photograph, taken in June 1913, is of such a party from a department of Messrs Ryland & Son of Wood Street, taking a break in the pub's paddock.

Although regular stagecoach services had ceased many years earlier, this coach and its horses were taken out of retirement as a tourist special, running past The Pheasant on a daily journey between Great Missenden and Windsor during the summer season just before the First World War. This was one of two coach routes operated for visitors in the Misbourne valley; the other ran between Wendover and Rickmansworth, also a run of nearly 20 miles. The fare for that distance was 7s 6d single, or 12s 6d return, plus an extra half-crown for the privilege of a box seat up with the coachman.

Posted in 1919 this card shows a typical motorist of the period taking his family for a spin. Beyond the covered wagon is the beginning of housing growth along the main road to Chalfont St Peter. The newly formed Penn Country branch of the Council for the Preservation of Rural England fought hard to restrict such ribbon development.

Published by the landlord as an advertisement, this card is postmarked 1938. The Pheasant is now featuring a different brewer, Benskins, which had taken over the Amersham Brewery and Weller's tied houses in 1929. They still made a feature of the Tea Rooms and Gardens, with an entrance behind the building in Pheasant Hill, the road to the village.

More recently, this 1960 card shows a smartly painted Pheasant on a much busier road. Widening of the main road and the Vache Lane corner had necessitated the demolition of The Nook. The redundant horse-trough has disappeared and a small car park has been built where a barn and stables once stood.

VISIT THE **Pheasant** $\mathbf{I}$**nn** ST. GILES
when you are

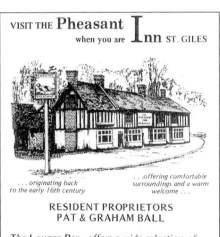

... originating back
to the early 16th century

...offering comfortable
surroundings and a warm
welcome...

RESIDENT PROPRIETORS
PAT & GRAHAM BALL

The Lounge Bar - offers a wide selection of
Hot & Cold Snacks
& TRADITIONAL CASK ALES
The Cromwell Room Restaurant - amidst the
history of 'Oliver Cromwell' who came to the
village of St. Giles in 1642 - a fine cellar of
wines accompanies a well balanced
a la carte menu
The Garden & Paddock - overlooking Silsden
Mead and the village with its
Church and Duck Pond —
fully licenced bar - childrens shop & tuckin —
evening Bar-B-Ques — adventure play area —
garden terrace for adults to relax in whilst
children may play away in safety.

Finally, this advertisement was published in the Official Guide to the Parish Church in 1980. But that is not quite the end of its story, for in 1995 The Pheasant suffered the ultimate indignity, when a restaurant chain took over and changed the historic name. After numerous complaints from patrons and the Parish Council, tradition prevailed and the original name was restored.

Two
Valley of the Misbourne

Near, CHALFONT St GILES.
Bucks.

The River Misbourne rises above Great Missenden and flows through Little Missenden and Old Amersham before reaching Chalfont St Giles. In past centuries there was sufficient water to power six watermills in the eight miles before Chalfont Mill, but abstraction to meet the growing demands for water throughout the twentieth century severely reduced the river's flow. This, together with the naturally intermittent behaviour of chalk streams, resulted in long periods without water after dry seasons, particularly in the section through Chalfont St Giles, although it often re-appeared further downstream. The anonymous painter of this scene, published in 1900, has used artistic licence in the inclusion of a church tower near the crest of the hill, but the general impression is typical of the Misbourne when it is flowing, with willow trees on the crumbling bank of a stream of crystal clear water.

Believed to be the oldest mill site in Buckinghamshire, dating from the sixteenth century, Chalfont Mill was being used as an electricity generating station in 1905, the date of this card. The tall chimney indicates reliance on steam power when flow was insufficient to turn the mill-wheel. The stream below the mill and the adjacent fields were then also in use for the rearing of Aylesbury ducks.

This photograph was taken in 1911 by a member of the Greenford Cycling Club, showing a colleague negotiating the ford in Mill Lane. On this occasion the Misbourne was flowing particularly well, with the water level almost up to the footbridge alongside the mill.

The view, taken in 1915, of the Misbourne valley from the Amersham Road included Stratton Chase, the mansion among the trees near the crest of the hill. Its estate included most of the pictured land on the further slope. The river is hidden by the line of trees across the middle of the scene with the mill at the bottom of the strip of dark conifers.

Described in a guide of 1905 as 'recently built by Mr Gurney', Stratton Chase, pictured here just after the First World War, was an extravagant mansion constructed on a grand scale, with equally grand conservatories, all fronted by a terraced lawn giving views over the valley.

The back of the house, with another conservatory, is shown on this 1910 postcard. The formal flower beds and kitchen garden behind the house were on land originally cleared from Perry Field Plantation.

Looking back from the drive c. 1910. This view gives another impression of the sheer size of the mansion. The drive is nearly three quarters of a mile long to Chalfont St Giles, lined with well-trimmed beech hedges near the house and an avenue of trees nearer the village. Barely twenty years old, the house was destroyed by fire in 1921.

In this 1915 view up Pheasant Hill, the road is shaded by the elms in the grounds of The Stone, which lie behind the brick wall on the left. On the other side of the road, Stone Meadow, an unofficial public open space, extends to the garden and paddock of The Pheasant, at the top of the slope.

Looking down Pheasant Hill c. 1935. The gate near the edge of the picture leads to the stables of The Stone, an 1810 replacement for the historic house of that name where Oliver Cromwell stayed during the Civil War. The new house is at the top of the grounds whereas the original was down by the river, near the stables.

Looking down the well-cropped grass to Chalfont St Giles church around 1915, Stone Meadow is an essential extension of the open countryside into the heart of the village. Since 1937 this view and the peaceful setting have been under threat from a proposal to divert the main Amersham Road through the meadow.

In this 1925 photograph the Misbourne is about the size seen under favourable conditions today, but a mere trickle compared to the beginning of the century and now insufficient to turn any mill wheel, meandering between grassy banks and aged willow trees.

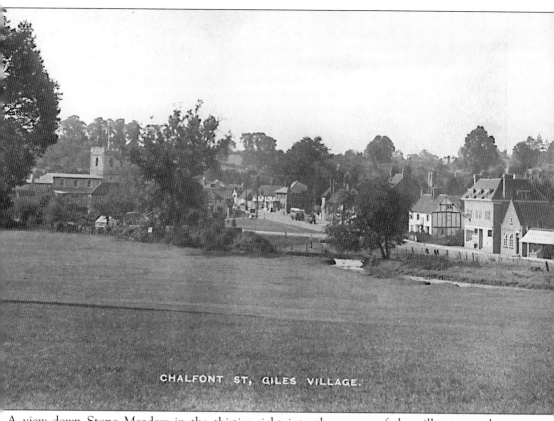

CHALFONT ST, GILES VILLAGE.

A view down Stone Meadow in the thirties right into the centre of the village over the Misbourne and the hidden pond emphasises the open aspect of the village. The Misbourne passes under the road from The Stone's stables and runs through the corner of the meadow, where it is now crossed by a footbridge consisting of a single Sarsen stone slab over its six-foot width. Stone Meadow is the traditional venue for the Chalfont St Giles Show, an annual event combining competitive displays of horticultural and domestic produce with entertainments for adults and fun and games for the children.

A large proportion of the village population, which then numbered some 1,400, sat down in their Sunday best to a celebration meal served at lines of tables outside marquees set up

on the bottom of Stone Meadow, on the occasion of the Coronation of King Edward VII in June 1902.

Photographed just after the Second World War from the Meadow, the river, wider but shallower after passing the pond, here skirts the churchyard and flows under a wooden bridge carrying the footpath from the church to the eastern edge of the parish.

Looking across the river from near the churchyard, c. 1925. The main Uxbridge Road at the top of the meadow is already lined with houses and bungalows. The cows are drinking in a stretch of the river which, a hundred years earlier, widened into a lake and was used as a fishery.

Three
The Village Pond

Chalfont St Giles pond, with the bordering cottages and church tower reflected in the water, is the epitome of the old English village. This scene might be regarded as the trade-mark of Chalfont St Giles, the scene by which it is instantly recognized, as it was an extremely popular subject with both artists and photographers, so that about a quarter of all postcards of the village depict the pond. This view was painted by the popular postcard artist 'Jotter', Walter Hayward Young, and published in 1900. The pond, fed from the intermittent Misbourne stream, is also liable to level fluctuations and occasional dry periods, but such is its importance to the village that alternative sources were provided to top it up when necessary. The following views in this chapter show the changes to the pond and its surroundings through the twentieth century.

CHALFONT ST GILES.

COLES Watford.

From approximately the same date, a Watford photographer has here captured the same scene, complete with swans, also reflected in the still water. The lumbering traction engine in the High Street has managed to move enough to appear blurred during the time exposure then needed by photographic plates.

Chalfont St. Giles, near Rickmansworth.

Pictured by a Rickmansworth photographer around 1910, a horse-drawn cart is in the shallow water where the horse can take a refreshing drink whilst cooling his hooves. The writer of the card referred to Chalfont St Giles as a real country place, but complained that he had to go miles for his shopping.

When pictured in 1915, with low water in the pond and a smoke haze hanging over the buildings near the church, the 'Duke of Wellington', the timbered building to the right of the pond, was then coming to the end of its life as a public house. The trees in the background are on the high ground which almost encircles Chalfont St Giles, the river valley being the only level access.

By the late twenties, with less horse traffic and reduced demands as a drinking trough, parts of the pond had become choked with reeds. The village was still virtually deserted, but what little traffic there was then consisted of motor vans.

Taken around 1930, this view from the meadow shows how near the pond is to the river, which should keep it topped up. The river dried up through the last years of the twentieth century until, at the start of 2001, after excessive rainfall, it not only filled the pond but also engulfed the houses and shops around the green.

This postcard dates from the thirties, but with a lone cow beside the pond and no visible traffic or pedestrians, the scene is virtually timeless. The only changes from the earliest pictures of the village are minor alterations of detail such as shop fronts, with no new buildings or major alterations to the old ones.

By 1940 a pavement had been laid alongside the road past the weed-covered pond, and a grassy bank had re-formed by the water's edge except where small children, like this lone boy in full school uniform, have worn it away.

In this postcard, published around 1950, the pond is protected by a double chain barrier, with a concrete edged sluice built to control the water level, where it can overflow when well filled from the river, or be topped up by water pumped from a well in dry spells.

Four
The Village Green

This view of the green over the rooftops of Church Cottages was taken from the church tower in the late twenties. Until 1930 the green was bisected by a service track directly opposite the Merlins Cave, but this was then removed and the green unified into a single stretch of grass, later carrying the village sign and occasionally, when Chalfont St Giles had been successful in its class, the County's Best Kept Village sign. The green is officially a part of the High Street and both sides include the first shops of the 'one long straggling street' as an early twentieth century guide described the village. The chapter begins with views of the green itself, then the buildings on the road side, followed by those behind the greensward.

This postcard view of the green, c. 1905, includes part of the pond where a goose appears to have taken a dislike to the photographer. The green, then fenced by wires between short posts, was deserted, but there was plenty of activity in the High Street.

The green is pictured here in the mid thirties, after the middle track had been restored to grass and the whole edged with kerbstones. Here a delivery van waits outside the hardware shop, while a city gent parks his bicycle outside William Green's shoe repair shop. A single hand-operated petrol pump stands way off the road, outside the small house next to the Merlins Cave.

In the late forties the cycle and hardware shop has most of its stock on the pavement outside its own premises and those of 'Paynes Stores' next door. Paynes was a multi-purpose shop, combining hairdressing with the sale of tobacco, stationery, toys and fancy goods and the publication of postcards.

To commemorate the 1953 Coronation, the village sign, a painting of the legendary St Giles, was unveiled on the corner of the green by the eminent judge, Sir Norman Birkett, a local resident. This view dates from the late fifties, and includes the three Church Cottages, or correctly, Dame Clayton's Almshouses, facing the green in front of the church tower.

This close-up of Chalfont St Giles village sign was photographed around 1960 and shows the detail of the painting. It depicts Aegidus, a seventh-century hermit who protected a hind being chased by the Royal hunt, and took in his own arm an arrow aimed at the animal. He was later canonized as St Giles, the patron saint of woodland animals, beggars and the sick.

The first shops and houses facing the green, c. 1910. The line of buildings, of various dates and in various styles, starts with the late Victorian shop of James Sears, which had only recently become the fourth home of Chalfont St Giles post office.

44

A more detailed picture of the post office shortly after it opened, this card was sent by a post office employee in October 1909 to show where he then worked. Two telegram boys, one with his delivery cycle, stand outside together with the counter staff. Next door, beyond the shop, is the Duke of Wellington, and beyond that again, a horse waits patiently near his cart in the field alongside the ancient tithe barn.

Looking back from the top of the green past the same line of buildings, c. 1910. The vine-covered building was the bakehouse of Ernest Stacey, who had baked the village's bread since the closing years of the nineteenth century.

At the back of the shop, Stacey's opened a tea room, serving their home-made cakes and pastries. It started in 1901, apparently to feed the large number of visiting worshippers who came to hear a particularly charismatic preacher. Pictured in its early years, the tea rooms remained open until the difficulties of rationing forced closure in 1941.

The Village, Chalfont, St Giles, showing the Tea-Rooms & Pump.

Despite the title of this 1915 postcard, the tea room is hardly discernible, but the pump is very obvious in the middle of the road, surrounded by small boys, only one of whom stood still long enough for the photograph. At the extreme left edge, the brick pillar holds the entrance gate to Stratton Court Drive.

STRATTON LANE, CHALFONT ST. GILES.

Pictured around 1930, around half a mile from the site of Stratton Court, the Drive, now called Stratton Lane, slopes down to the gateway facing the green. Shortly after its construction a guide book described the entrance as an imposing brick gateway out of keeping with the rest of the village.

Another part of the village's 1902 celebrations was this parade of horse-drawn carts carrying villagers

dressed up for the occasion past equally well-dressed onlookers outside the flag-bedecked cottages.

Here the pump has gained a new neighbour, a gas street lamp, in its vulnerable position in the middle of the road junction outside the bank. At this date, around 1918, it was still a daily necessity for many villagers without mains water, particularly those in the old cottages up Silver Hill, the turning opposite the pump.

This close-up of the pump was taken shortly before it was moved, in July 1920, to a safer position on the edge of the green. The council arranged for the move because it was often being knocked over by traffic, and its regular users had to put up with a dry day while the village plumber and his son carried out the move.

THE PUMP & GREEN, CHALFONT ST. GILES.

Taken shortly after the 1920 move, this view of the pump in its new wooden casing standing on the edge of the green also includes the rough track serving the premises behind the green. To the right of the track is the yard where Nash's Stores parked their delivery van, next to the creeper-covered end wall of the Church Houses.

THE OLD VILLAGE PUMP, CHALFONT ST. GILES.

About 1930 and the pump, no longer a necessity, has lost its wooden jacket. The service road has been surfaced and widened with kerbs and a pavement past the Merlins Cave and the shops beyond.

51

This 1894 cabinet photograph by an East London studio includes the neighbouring shops as well as the pub which had been 'recently rebuilt and enlarged in good taste by Messrs Weller' according to a guide book of the same date. One theory of the origin of the pub's name was that a cave had been found in the meadow behind it, another that it was suggested by Milton.

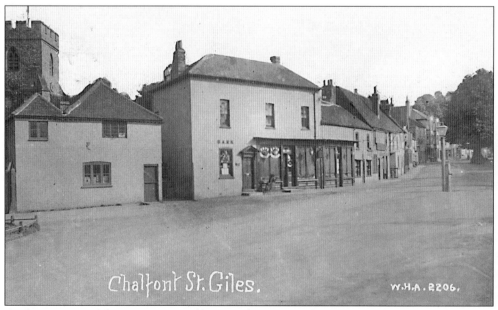

At the very top of the green, pictured here in about 1915, the premises adjoining the bank had a wide shop front grafted on by the expanding Nash's Stores. The passageway between the bank and the neighbouring cottages leads to the church, and the next chapter.

Five

St Giles Church

The parish church of St Giles is built of very thick flint walls with stone dressings under a flat-pitched lead-covered roof. It dates partly from the twelfth century, with various additions and alterations from every century since, culminating in a major Victorian restoration. The church contains the tombs and monuments of many of the important residents of The Vache, including Bishop Hare, Dean of St Paul's, who gave the fine seventeenth-century oak altar rails, believed to have been brought from the cathedral. In the fourteenth century the interior was covered in paintings but these were subsequently covered in a rough grey plaster, much of which was removed, together with some of the paintings, in the Victorian overhaul. A lot more was revealed by experts in the twenties and quite large areas are now on display. This view of the outside of the church dates from around 1900.

Entrance to Church, Chalfont St Giles.

Approaching by the narrow passage from the green, the first sight of the church is of its tower, seen between ancient yew trees on this postcard from the mid-thirties. The tower at the western end of the church was built, or rebuilt, in the fifteenth century, and its clock, originally with only one hand, was added in 1710.

Chalfont St. Giles Church

W.H.A. 2204.

On this 1915 postcard the south side of the church and the creeper-covered tower are seen over the graveyard. An 1896 guide refers to the exceptional beauty of the Virginia creeper in its autumn colours, but noted the overall unkempt appearance, still apparent twenty years later.

The village War Memorial towers above all the other stones and crosses, c. 1925. The writer of this card, while resting on the base of the War Memorial on her way home from the shops, describes it as 'the prettiest churchyard I have ever seen, always kept gay with cut flowers'.

The river makes a beautiful setting for the church, particularly with reflections in the slow moving water, as on this 1900 postcard. However, during its occasional periods of flood, it overflowed into the churchyard almost to the church door and swamped the boiler house, partly below floor level, necessitating the construction of a new boiler house, above ground, in 1960.

SOUTH GATE OF CHURCH, CHALFONT ST. GILES.

Pictured around 1930, this porch of solid English oak had been built over the south door of the church in 1895. The previous porch had rotted away and been removed in 1760, leaving the ancient ornamented door unprotected for well over a century.

Parish Church Chalfont St Giles.

The interior of the church is pictured in the mid-twenties, shortly before the hanging oil lamps were replaced by concealed electric lighting. Fragments of the ancient wall paintings had been revealed over the chancel arch, but much more, including a curious battlemented design extending the whole width, was expertly uncovered in 1929.

CHALFONT ST GILES,
THE LYCH GATE.

Pictured around 1930, another passage from the churchyard led out through this sixteenth-century rotating lych gate, between half-timbered buildings of the same period, into the High Street opposite the Crown Hotel. At one time a rope round the pulley on the shaft of the gate led to a counterweight holding the gate closed, but this had been removed as a danger to children.

37065 CHALFONT ST. GILES, LYCH GATE.
Seaull Co. Gerrards Cross

Looking back from the High Street c. 1915, the railings of the churchyard can be seen beyond the gate. The complete lych gate was moved in 1956 to an opening in the railings under its own tiled roof, leaving the archway unobstructed.

Six

High Street

This drawing of the main part of the High Street by Albert Foster is taken from his book *The Chiltern Hundreds*, published in 1897. The most noticeable landmark is the large tree, known as Milton's Elm, growing at the side of the road, where it remained a feature of the village until finally removed in 1940 as a hazard to traffic. The line of shops on the left hand side continues to the top of the street, but there are no buildings on the right beyond the elm, where the grounds of the old rectory border the road. In the early years of the twentieth century, writers of guide books remarked on the colour and character given to the street by the line of elm trees standing behind the rectory wall. The pictures in this chapter are arranged to show the buildings in sequence from the bottom of the street to the top.

Chalfont St. Giles from Green   Coles, Photographer, Wa

Looking up an almost deserted High Street from the top of the green, *c.* 1900. This view includes the pump with its usual complement of children. The Crown, on the right, advertised itself as 'The Most Comfortable Hotel in the Chalfont Country', offering luncheons, dinners and teas, catering for parties in private rooms, and 'of special convenience for cyclists'.

Before the Great War had ended, plans were prepared for a War Memorial in the middle of the High Street, near the pump, drawn here from nearly the same viewpoint as the previous photograph. The plan was later dropped and a simple stone cross was erected in the churchyard instead.

This view of the lych gate and neighbouring buildings was printed in an 1895 guide book, when they were still private houses. The first shop, slightly further up the street, was Charles Marchant's, which combined boot and shoe manufacture and repair with grocery. It was also the second home of the village post office.

Now a more detailed view of The Crown in its prominent position on the corner of High Street and Silver Hill, here decorated in celebration of the 1902 Coronation. In addition to bar doorways on the corner and in both streets, there was a private entrance for residential guests via the back door at the edge of the view.

By 1905 the post office had been separated from Marchant's shop and moved next door into one of the half-timbered cottages. No longer sharing a shop, this was its third location in the village. At this time the sight of a photographer, still a fairly unusual occurrence, was enough to bring many of the village children out to pose.

By the mid-thirties the house to the left of the lych-gate arch had become a newsagent's shop, known as Ye Olde Shoppe, referring to the sixteenth-century building, rather than Simpson's business there, which was quite new. Waiting opposite the green is an Amersham and District bus on route 6 from Three Households to Gerrards Cross. This card was sent home by a family staying in one of the village pubs, which they described as 'very old but comfortable'.

After several changes of ownership, but still looking the same, the former large shop has been separated into two, c. 1950. A note on the back of this postcard refers to 'My Brother Arthur's Shop' at Chalfont St Giles. Arthur Parker's grocery filled the larger part, with Windsors ladies outfitters in the smaller.

Looking down the street in about 1918, the butcher's shop adjoining The Crown has both a substantial porch and heavy sunblinds to protect the display in its wide open shop window. Beyond the shop and the side turning, and opposite the playing children, are the ornate wrought-iron gates of Stratton Chase.

Here the band of the local Friendly Society branch, the Loyal Milton Lodge of the Manchester Unity Independent Order of Oddfellows, has gathered in front of their huge banner for an impromptu photo-call on the pavement outside a public house in July 1907. On special occasions they held joint parades with the Old Treaty House Lodge of Uxbridge, who carried an even larger banner.

Looking down High Street to the green, c. 1940. The Feathers pub is on the left, separated from its rival, The Crown, by a stationery shop. The part of The Crown which formerly housed the landlord's butchers shop has long been changed to a more appropriate trade, as an off-licence. Down by the green, the double-deck bus is making a rare visit to the village.

On a fairly busy day in 1910, small children are still able to amble and play in the middle of High Street, and on the rough grass verge outside the Reading Room. The only blot on an otherwise attractive scene is the rash of auctioneer's posters which have accumulated on the outhouse between The Feathers and the Reading Room.

The Reading Room *c.* 1930. This sixteenth-century building, was originally one of the rectory's cottages built on the edge of its grounds. After use as an infants' schoolroom, at the end of the nineteenth century it became a meeting room, a library and a young men's club.

This local newspaper photograph from the fifties shows the Women's Institute market stall, then held every Friday outside the Reading Room. Serving the long queue of customers are WI members Mrs M. Wallis, Miss H. Johnston, Mrs M. Williams and Mrs E. Martin, all under the watchful eye of the market controller, Mrs L.C. Marx.

THE OLD ELM, CHALFONT ST. GILES

This postcard, sent with a birthday greeting in 1914, features the ancient elm tree known as Milton's Elm, still looking very healthy at the edge of the road just beyond the Reading Room.

Looking up the other side of the street opposite the Reading Room around 1905, we see a pair of neighbouring pubs belonging to rival breweries. The bay-windowed Sugar Loaves remained in business until the mid-thirties, but the Elm Tree closed around the beginning of the Great War. The usual group of children seated on the roots of Milton's Elm appear to be intently watching for something to appear in the part-glazed archway between the pubs.

106. HIGH STREET, CHALFONT ST. GILES.

A very quiet High Street is pictured in about 1910, but the notices beside the Feathers hint at the growth to come, advertising the auction of plots around the village for residential development, including the remaining 45 acres of Pollards Wood. The boards leaning against the front of the Feathers advertised various agricultural auctions, some of which were held in the pub.

Pictured on a bright sunny day in the twenties, the only life in the unsurfaced street is two horse-drawn vehicles, a light trap near the pump, and a heavy cart unloading goods at Marchant's shop. The Elm Tree pub had been closed for around ten years but still bears the wrought-iron bracket which once carried the name board above its former coach entrance.

Herbert Carter opened his bakery business in the twenties in the former Elm Tree pub. In this picture, taken shortly after opening, the proprietor and his wife are standing proudly by their smart new van parked outside the shop, which was destined to be demolished a few years later.

71

THE OLD ELM, CHALFONT ST. GILES.

R.A.P.C
London.

Pictured in the thirties, opposite the gnarled stump of the old Elm, Albert Warner had opened his butchers shop in a tall new building on the site of The Elm Tree pub, where the family business still remains. Later, when a petition was organized against the proposed removal of the last remaining part of the famous tree, the rapidly increasing list of names was displayed on the pictured face of the stump itself.

Pictured somewhere on his rounds, Warner's delivery boy, wearing a traditional striped apron, carries the meat orders in the basket of his cycle which also advertises a Rickmansworth branch.

In the late thirties Robert Moore could genuinely offer an express delivery service, as advertised on his motor-tricycle. He shared the telephone number 16 with Warner's butchers shop, with whom he must have worked in partnership, offering a faster service than the boy on the bike.

Herbert Carter had recently moved his bakery two doors up the street, to this distinctive building with square bays on all three floors, pictured here in the mid thirties. A couple of years later they opened the Elm Tree Tearooms at the back of the shop.

74

Milton's Elm, Chalfont St. Giles.

By 1932 Milton's Elm had been reduced to a mere stump, the gnarled roots of which still provided informal seating for the old folk of the village as they had done for generations. Even the stump was under threat by 1934, and despite vociferous protests and the 800-name petition, it was removed in 1940 as a hazard to passing traffic.

The last shop in High Street, pictured here in about 1920, was an ironmongers, keeping up the tradition of that trade by displaying part of his stock outside the front door. Next door, with the donkey cart outside, was a fishmonger's shop, run for over twenty-five years by the Rance family.

The Old Elm Tree. Chalfont St Giles.

Pictured in the early thirties, the right-hand shop had been taken over by the local Church Farm Dairy. On the other side of the road, many brick buttresses shore up the wall of the rectory garden which was bulging badly due to the pressure of the higher ground and the roots of the trees there.

CHALFONT ST. GILES.

At the top of High Street is the white painted seventeenth-century Anthony Cottage, pictured in the thirties when it was the office of Louis Worley, coal and coke merchant. The single-storey brick outhouse extended to the corner of Bowstridge Lane where it carried the street lamp. Later, the outhouse, which had become derelict, was removed to permit road widening.

76

Seven

Dean Way

Dean or Dene Way, the continuation of High Street, climbs gently in its own little valley (or dene). Its only important feature is an unpretentious late sixteenth-century cottage, probably built for the Fleetwood family of The Vache. John Milton, the poet, lived there for a while in 1665-6 as a refuge from London when the Great Plague was at its height. This is the only one of his homes still standing, and is now a place of pilgrimage for devotees of English poetry from all over the world. When Milton lived here, it was the last house in the village, and it still gives that impression as a large tree-lined field separates the cottage from later development further out. In this 1910 picture taken from the top of the field, Milton's Cottage and its neighbours in Dean Way lie across the centre of the view.

Resuming the tour of Chalfont St Giles at the top of High Street, this 1950 postcard shows the sixteenth-century Stonewell Farm, the oldest house in the village, at the corner of Bowstridge Lane and Dean Way, and, beyond it, the terrace of cottages leading up to Milton's.

This card from around 1925 of one wing of Stonewell Farm, then in very poor condition, also includes part of its grounds stretching up the slope beside the lane. Large granite blocks found in the garden of the farmhouse are believed to be from the original stone well, probably of the Roman period.

Behind Stonewell Farm, at the crest of the hill is the aptly named Hill House, commanding wide views across the centre of the village. In this late Victorian or Edwardian photograph, three ladies of the household pose in the porch, which is of the same ogee shape as the sash windows on either side.

This was the view, taken around 1930, from the allotment gardens slightly below Hill House on the opposite side of Bowstridge Lane, but still at the same height as the top of the church tower. The ground drops away surprisingly steeply to the cottages and outbuildings behind the High Street shops. Today this view is hidden by housing development on the field.

BREAKSPEARE'S FARM CHALFONT ST GILES

Returning to Dean Way, this card of the creeper-clad front of Stonewell Farm dates from the beginning of the twentieth century. The right-hand wing was then the butcher's shop of William Elliot Nash, farmer and former surveyor of highways. Around the direction boards the plaster is beginning to show signs of its age, as is the roof. In addition to the title used on this card, the building was occasionally called Shakespeare's Farm.

Photographed again in the thirties when the occupants of three cars are visiting Milton's Cottage which had been open to the public as a museum of Milton's life since it was bought in 1897 by public subscription including a significant contribution from Queen Victoria. This was prompted by an American official's offer to buy and transport the building. The notice on the street face of the chimney advises admission charges of 6d each, or a party rate of 1s 3d for three.

This drawing of the front garden of Milton's Cottage dates from the early 1800s and was used in a book published in 1895. It shows the house as it must have been in Milton's time, with a strange two-storey porch over the front door.

This rather stark view of the front of Milton's Cottage was photographed in 1900. The porch had been demolished, the front door moved and the large chimney abutting the street rebuilt in about 1850, but the interior of the cottage remained virtually unaltered.

In about 1910, a softer impression is created after restoration of the garden with neat flower beds and well-trimmed grass around the blossoming fruit trees, a perfect setting for a typical English cottage. The poet's study is to the right of the front door, and the kitchen, with its long low window, to the left.

Inside the cottage, two rooms, the poet's study and the kitchen, were turned into a small museum of Milton relics, including precious first editions of his works, together with examples of local arts and crafts. This 1910 view of the poet's study shows his desk in front of the open fireplace.

View of the old kitchen, bright with daylight through the familiar narrow window, *c.* 1910. The enormous fireplace, which opens into the outside chimney stack, contains many of the implements of two and a half centuries earlier, and the glass cabinets hold further items of the valuable collection.

This card was sent in 1912 as 'another card for your album, hope you like it'. Milton's Cottage lies in the dip at the bottom of the field then occupied by a family of pigs. Also, on the left of the view, the Victorian buildings of the village school can just be seen between the trees on the hillside opposite the cottage.

MILTON VIEW (Opposite Milton Cottage, Chalfont St. Giles).
Large or small Parties catered for in or out doors.—W. J. CARDEN.
Telegrams: CARDEN, CHALFONT ST. GILES.

A nineteenth-century book on the homes of eminent British poets refers to a wheelwright's house and yard in a dell opposite Milton's Cottage, but from about 1900 the Milton View restaurant stood on the sloping site across the road. Pictured here in its early years from a window of the cottage, this card was sent by the restaurant's proprietor requesting details of the Wycombe.

This advertisement was published in a 1930 guide to The Chalfont Country after a new hostess had taken over and changed the name. Several guides and ramblers' handbooks of the twenties and thirties, when describing Milton's Cottage, referred to the proximity of a good tea-room.

MILTON HALT
(OPPOSITE MILTON'S COTTAGE)

CHALFONT ST. GILES

R.A.C. Restaurant.

GUEST HOUSE & RESTAURANT

Terms : 7/6 per Day.

Within two miles of Jordan's Friends'
Meeting House.

Stations :
GERRARDS CROSS, MARYLEBONE AND PADDINGTON.

Hostess :   *Telephone :*
E. BICKER-CAARTEN.   Chalfont St. Giles **172**.

Standing well above the road, a few doors along from Milton View, the Congregational Church was built in 1854. This postcard was published shortly after the building was re-fronted in 1901. After the 1977 merger with the Methodists from just up the road, this building was redundant and has since been replaced by a residential home on the site.

Posted in 1911, this card shows Dean Way looking back past the tree-edged field next to Milton's Cottage. Outside the Milton's Head an AA traffic notice gives very advance warning of the presence of the school in the side turning beyond Milton View.

This advertising card from around 1960 shows the enlarged Milton Head, with the remains of two painted signs just legible between the upstairs windows. Below these, large bays and a covered entrance porch have replaced the previous wooden verandah.

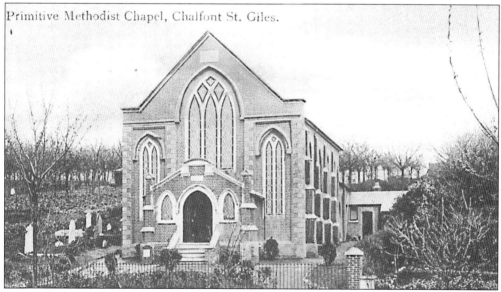

A little further up Dean Way the Primitive Methodist Chapel was photographed from the field across the road. After open-air meetings from 1832 the first chapel was opened here in 1847. The current chapel was built in 1866 and the picture dates from immediately after its renovation, with a new porch, in 1905.

Again looking back down Dean Way, the Methodist Chapel, on the bank above the road, dominates this 1925 view, with the minister's house, Danebury, this side of it behind the decorative wall. After the union of the Methodist and United Free (formerly Congregational) churches, this chapel was chosen to serve the combined congregation as Deanway United Church.

Now turning up Dean Way at the same date and from the same viewpoint, on the right is the block of 4 Deanway Cottages, and the pair of Orchard Cottages, hardly recognizable today after the addition of large front extensions. The first dark roadside building then housed Bleach's boot shop, and the other, behind it was the Fleetwood Stores.

Eight

Three Households

The top end of Dean Way leads directly into the uniquely named Three Households, a hamlet at the edge of Chalfont St Giles, still small but with considerably more than the original three families. Despite its rural location, in Victorian times it boasted an iron foundry, and alongside the usual farmers, shopkeepers and beer sellers, the employment listed in local directories included blacksmith, coal merchant, chimney sweep, pheasant breeder, sieve maker, wheelwright, and two chair-makers.

The hamlet's name originated when one building, believed to have been a single dwelling, was sub-divided to accommodate three households. The name was later given to the road past the building, then applied to the community as a whole. This photo of the original building was taken in the twenties when two of the houses incorporated shops.

At the end of Dean Way, entering Three Households, the first building is the 'White Hart', a large public house on the corner of Back Lane. This card was used in 1906 by the landlord, Joseph Birch, to order '2 dozen syphons of Soda' from mineral water manufacturers Wallingtons, of The Rose & Crown in Waterside, Chesham.

On the next corner, beside the turning for Chalfont St Peter, was another pub, Uncle Tom's Cabin, pictured here in the twenties. The landlord George Smith, who had previously been a shopkeeper elsewhere in the hamlet, presided over the hostelry from around 1910 until the Second World War.

In 1912 the Royal Commission on Historical Monuments had reported on the seventeenth-century 'Three Households' building, noting that one of the end cottages was in a bad condition with decaying timbers and much ivy. On this card of around 1920, looking back past other houses, to the end of the divided building with its original brick chimney, the exposed timbers are still in poor condition.

In this view from the forties, the original Three Households have been restored, with tile-hanging to protect the timbers of the front. Miss Tripp's General Store, occupying two of the cottages, faces the rival Home Farm Stores across the road.

Bowles Farm.

At the far end of Three Households, Bowles Farm stands at a bend in the road, with its orchards behind it. In this 1905 postcard view, seen from the entrance to the neighbouring smithy, the farmhouse is partly hidden by an outbuilding in front of the four Bowles Farm Cottages, originally built for its farmworkers.

Until the orchards were cut down, mainly for housing development, the area around Chalfont St Giles, particularly at this end of the village, was famous for its cherries, and for the display of spring blossom. This press photograph from the late thirties conveys the beauty of the gnarled old trees on a local farm.

94

Nine
Old Jordans

From Three Households, Twitchells Lane continues as Jordans Lane, passing Old Jordans Farm, from which the surrounding area, including the twentieth century village, takes its name. From 1659 local Quakers met regularly at the farm for worship, suffering much persecution when caught by the local magistrates, until the Toleration Act of 1688 legalized such gatherings. Immediately after this the Quakers built their Meeting House just down the road. In the twentieth century, to keep a haven of peace and quiet around the Meeting House, Quakers bought Old Jordans and converted the farm and outbuildings into a hostel where Friends and others could stay away from the bustle and noise of regular life. On this yard from the early twenties the barns stand behind the orchard to the left of the main hostel building, the extended Old Jordans farmhouse.

This was Jordans Lane in around 1905, when Old Jordans was still a farm and well before Jordans Village was even thought of. Old Jordans is about a hundred yards beyond the bend in the lane, and the lady is standing at the end of the footpath from Seer Green which eventually became Seer Green Lane, the entrance to the new village.

Old Jordans Farm was bought by the Society of Friends in 1911 and converted into a hostel providing rest and inspiration for private guests and small groups. It was so popular that a new wing was added by 1920. This 1925 view of the entrance from Jordans Lane includes the new wing to the left of the original farmhouse.

This detailed view of the old farmhouse was posted in 1912, and shows it in the first year after its restoration and conversion. The hostel visitors were then taking tea on the small terrace between the main building and the turreted annexe. At the left edge of the picture, the roof of the Mayflower Barn can be seen over the corner of the farm's seventeenth-century granary.

Published around 1915, this postcard shows the kitchen of the old farm, then in use as the hostel dining room, with a highly polished wooden table and Windsor chairs. This room, an addition in 1618 to the original building, is where the early Quakers met for worship.

This card of the interior of the hostel was posted in 1925. A note on the back records that: 'The Ingle Nook was discovered and restored in 1922. It is the oldest part of the Hostel and is known to have been in existence in the 16th century. Originally it was the outer wall of the building'.

This 1930 view of tea-time on the lawn was taken from the open door of the Mayflower Barn. To the left of the lawn is the refectory, its extended roof slope providing a wide verandah the length of the building. The garden furniture is a mixture of folding deck chairs and traditional Windsor style chairs probably made in one of the many furniture factories in High Wycombe.

The old farm stables alongside Jordans Lane had been converted into the refectory, described as 'one long reception room with attics'. Pictured here in about 1940 from the lane, the refectory was burnt down in 1962 and replaced a few years later by a new building in similar style.

On the southern side of the former farmyard stands the massive farm barn, a well-preserved example of a Buckinghamshire barn, built in 1624, using second-hand ship's timbers, believed to have come from the Pilgrim Fathers' ship, the *Mayflower*. On this postcard from the early years of the hostel, the barn is seen over the newly established garden and lawn.

A companion card shows the inside of the barn with its salt-impregnated timbers, many of which have bolt holes remaining from their previous use. The raised threshing floor at one end provided a stage for later musical and theatrical presentations.

THE GARDENER'S COTTAGE, OLD JORDANS HOSTEL.   10440

Pictured in the forties the Gardener's Cottage stands in its own attractive garden, behind the Mayflower Barn at the edge of the hostel grounds, and is now used as overflow accommodation for hostel visitors.

Another card from the forties shows the hostel as seen from the adjacent orchard which flanks two sides of the Old Jordans farm complex. From the hostel a path through the orchard provides a quieter alternative to Jordans Lane as a route to the Meeting House.

Published in 1915, this card shows The Dell, a former lime-pit, and part of the 'plot of ground called Well Close, together with the Dell of Wood therein' purchased by the Friends in 1688, on which to build the Meeting House. Included in the view is the well from which the plot of land was named.

Immediately after buying the land, the Friends set about building their Meeting House, the craftsmen using local materials wherever possible, including roof-tiles probably from Tylers Green. It was completed incredibly quickly, the first prayer meeting taking place within six months of the purchase. Published around 1910 this postcard view shows the Meeting House with its background of trees.

The Meeting House, initially known as New Jordans to avoid confusion with the farm just up the lane, c. 1920. Two thirds of the building is the actual Meeting Room, but the near end is the two-storey cottage of the caretaker. The back section contains the original stables with a more recent addition above.

JORDONS MEETING HOUSE & GALLERY.   10441

Inside, the white-washed walls of the Meeting House are partly panelled in deal, with simple wooden benches for a total of about 150 worshippers, on a plain brick floor. At the back of the room removable panels, open in this 1950 view, allow the study, main bedroom and kitchen of the caretakers house to be used as galleries for additional worshippers.

THE STABLES, JORDANS.   Downer, Watford.

This 1900 postcard shows the interior of the stables at the back of the Meeting House. In such an isolated position, and drawing members from miles around, stables were very much a necessity in the early days, and the stalls could house twenty horses while their owners were at prayer.

104

The adjacent graveyard was first used several years before the Meeting House was built. Although very simple headstones were used to mark the graves, Quaker attitude to such 'undue worldliness' hardened and they were removed in 1766. The layout was recorded (from memory) in 1798 and, after a change of attitude, replacement stones were erected in 1862. The stone on the left marks the grave of William Penn, founder of the colony, later state, of Pennsylvania.

The main entrance to the Meeting House grounds is on the corner of Jordans Lane and Welders Lane. This card was posted by a visitor in 1919, who wrote 'I am having a lovely restful time in beautiful surroundings. Jordans is one of the prettiest places I have seen, beautiful woods and fields, quiet country, and no street lamp to be seen, I am sure it will put me right again'.

This card, sent in 1908 by 'one of the campers at Jordans' shows a none-too-enthusiastic catering team beside their makeshift stoves and cauldrons some twenty years before the opening of a proper youth hostel at Jordans. Camping was permitted in the Meeting House grounds until well after the opening of the youth hostel, which provided beds for members of its association at a shilling a night for adults, half price for those under sixteen.

This card, published a few years later, shows Jordans Youth Hostel, opened in 1932 on a plot of land behind the Meeting House in Welders Lane. The simple building was constructed by Friends in Jordans Village and presented to the Youth Hostels Association, soon becoming one of the most popular hostels in their south-east region.

Dean Farm, dating from around 1520, but on a site occupied 300 years earlier, and with strong Quaker connections, stands on the other side of Jordans Lane from the Meeting House. Pictured from Longbottom Lane in 1900, it was then occupied by retired chair-maker Ebenezer Worley but formed part of the Wilton Park Estate.

Jordans Lane continues past the Meeting House and over the railway at Pot Kiln Lane, which takes its name from the Beaconsfield Pottery, later Brick and Tile Works, further along the road. This view from the forties includes a group of scouts striding out, probably eager to reach the Youth Hostel.

Pot Kiln Lane continues between woods for a straight mile to its junction with the main Oxford Road between Gerrards Cross and Beaconsfield. That junction is pictured on this 1910 postcard, looking towards Beaconsfield with Pot Kiln Lane to the right beside the white gates, a back entrance to Wilton Park.

Ten

Jordans Village

The fields of Dean Farm, alongside Jordans Lane opposite Old Jordans, were purchased in 1918 by a committee of Quakers to prevent speculative housing development which threatened the essential peace and quiet of the Meeting House and Hostel. Instead, they planned a new village as a 'self-governing human community in line with the Friends' principles', on the further fields, leaving an oasis of calm near those buildings. Part of the old footpath from Jordans Lane to Seer Green became Seer Green Lane, the entrance to the new Jordans Village, which was built steadily over the next ten years. Old Jordans hostel is in the centre of this 1925 aerial view, with the growing village in the big field to the left.

The Village, Jordans.

Back on the ground, this photograph also dates from 1925, when the first phase of the planned village development was completed, to the designs of Frederick Rowntree, architect, Quaker and chocolate baron. It shows the entrance to the village seen from Jordans Lane.

Seer Green Lane continues through the new village, forming the southern edge of the village green, a three-acre grass recreation space with children's swings and a see-saw. Pictured in the late twenties, the building on the corner of the green had been the builders' site office, becoming a temporary village shop in 1921 and finally the Estate Office.

This first terrace of cottages, facing the west side of the village green and known simply as 'A Group' was completed in 1919 and is pictured here the following year. A deposit of brick-earth had been found on the village site, but a kiln set up to produce the required bricks was hindered by a shortage of coal for firing.

A few years later and a more lived-in 'Green West Road' is complete with a cat by the first open gate. At the far end of the terrace, the wooden hut by the roadside had been brought second-hand from Bedford, re-erected and fitted out by village craftsmen in 1924 as the first permanent Jordans Co-operative Store who published this card soon afterwards.

In this early thirties view across its north-west corner, the green is now edged with a line of young birch trees. A large building had recently been erected between the first block of cottages and the village store. Built at the expense of two charitable Jordans residents, it is 'The Ark', a holiday home for children from London's East End.

The Village Green was not only an area for informal recreation and relaxation, it was the home of Jordans Cricket Club, in action in this picture from a late sixties guide to the district. Their presence was not, however, universally appreciated, and in the eighties a neighbouring resident demanded the erection of large screens to protect his property from stray balls.

POST OFFICE, JORDANS.

By the mid-thirties the roads had been thoroughly completed with a proper surface and edged with kerb stones. The final 1930 brick-built Village Stores and Post Office building stands next to The Ark with a telephone box outside. Although owned by a group of villagers who were also its principal customers, and therefore co-operative in the truest meaning of the word, 'co-operative' was dropped from the shop's title in 1934 as, to many, it implied a tie-up with the national Co-op.

PUERS LANE, JORDANS.

Green Road West continued north as Puers Lane, pictured here in the mid-thirties, where the detached houses contrast with the five groups of small cottages built for leasing to the craftsmen and artisans initially employed by Jordans Village Industries. These individual plots were limited to a maximum of one acre and then only if they were cultivated for fruit and vegetables.

Crutches Wood to the south-west of Jordans Village, a typical Buckinghamshire wood of mainly beech trees, was bought by contributions from wealthy Friends, dedicated in 1940, and 'permanently preserved in trust as an open space'. This postcard was published specially for the Village Store in around 1925.

114

This card, postmarked 1923, shows one of the pits in Crutches Wood, where some of the raw materials for building were obtained, but here in use as a playground. In the following year the Tenants Management Committee organised, as part of their traditional Midsummer Festival, a pastoral play in the amphitheatre of this exhausted gravel pit.

Pictured in the twenties, this is the well-worn path, later made up as Beech Lane, which drops gently through Crutches Wood to Long Bottom Lane, the road to Beaconsfield. Even before surfacing, it was regularly used as a short cut to Seer Green station.

Another 1925 aerial view showing the whole of the new Village area, with Crutches Wood at its heart. The initial development around the village green is seen at the top centre, above the wood, with further new houses on large plots both on Wilton Lane, to the left of the wood, and on Beech Lane where it emerges below the wood. The original buildings of Dean Farm are halfway up the right hand side of the photograph, and the railway, in its cutting, runs across the lower part of the view, with Jordans station just out of sight at the bottom edge.

This picture, another in the series published by the Village Store in 1925, shows the properties in Beech Lane at the southern edge of Crutches Wood in more detail. All, including the wooden hut, second from left, have well-cultivated gardens.

The White Cottage
Jordans. Bucks.

After emerging from Crutches Wood, Beech Lane continues past this distinctive thatched cottage with white painted walls, on its way down to the bottom of the valley. This sketch of the cottage was produced in 1932.

This last picture of Jordans village is a companion to the previous view, continuing the scene to the left, where Beech Lane passes in front of White Cottage and behind a large plot reserved for horticultural use. The photo was taken from Farm Lane, once the main route through Wilton Park to Beaconsfield, but cut short at the railway as Seer Green Station Road.

Beaconsfield Golf Club was opened within the grounds of Wilton Park beyond the railway line in 1914, boasting a luxurious, and above all convenient club-house, with its own railway halt only yards away. The course, in 200 acres of wooded country, was considered one of the best within easy reach of London. This view of the club-house dates from the thirties.

The railway opened in 1906 through the Longbottom valley, but the nearest stations were at Gerrards Cross and Beaconsfield until Beaconsfield Golf Club Halt was opened in 1915, when Miss Chrissy Childs, featured in this press photograph, was in sole charge of the station.

Wilton Park Estate included all the land between Longbottom Lane and the Oxford Road, and even without Dean Farm and the golf course covered the best part of two square miles of woods and parkland and the front and back drives were both a mile long. These two cards from the twenties show the front and back of the mansion, built or rebuilt in 1704. The estate was taken over by the army and used as a prisoner-of-war camp and interrogation centre during the Second World War. Then, while used by the Royal Army Education Corps, the Defence Ministry, in an act of wanton vandalism, demolished the mansion in 1967, replacing it with a hideous tower block and other tasteless buildings.

Eleven

Seer Green

The Church and Village, Seer Green.

Until the twentieth century, Seer Green consisted of little more than the 1846 church on the green, surrounded by a handful of cottages and two pubs, plus a few scattered farms, with a total population of about 300. By 1920 it had grown to about 400, then development started in earnest, reaching a peak in about 1930. when a writer described Seer Green as still a little country village with orchards between the cottages, and rickyards bordering the village street. He noted with dismay the estate developers' giant hoardings near Seer Green Halt, which spoiled the very rural setting they were promoting to potential home-buyers. Thankfully the village centre, photographed here in 1930, remained completely unspoilt despite the development all around.

In a small way, development had started in Seer Green in the early 1900s as an extension of neighbouring Beaconsfield, after the opening of the Railway Station there. The first executive commuters mostly settled in new houses on the wooded slopes of Long Bottom, and Seer Green House, pictured in around 1915, is a typical example of the houses built at that time, which later became a finishing school.

The road through Long Grove Wood was first developed in the twenties, with a few scattered large properties in individual clearings in the wood. Pictured in around 1950, later building, particularly at the northern end, nearer to the village centre, had resulted in the loss of all but a small vestige of the wood.

Orchard Road, Seer Green

This photograph from around 1950 includes the bakery of Milton Cromwell Lofty, renowned since before the First World War for his local cherry pies. Orchard Road, once noted for the cherry orchards on both sides, had been built up from 1925 onwards, with houses almost into the old centre of the village.

Church Road, Seer Green

Orchard Road continues past the Three Horseshoes, bordering one side of the former green. Church Road, pictured here from the pub forecourt in the fifties, forms another side. The first cottage, the post office and general store, with its telephone box almost hidden among the roadside trees, was well known for its black cherries, grown in the orchard behind the cottage.

Also seen from the pub forecourt, this 1930 view along the last section of Orchard Road, under the shade of a huge cedar tree in the churchyard, includes one of the Rose Cottages also built on the green. Beyond that is the 1899 Baptist Church in Chalfont Road, which was made redundant just before its centenary.

The Jubilee Well, with its protective cover of corrugated iron, standing on part of Rose Cottages front gardens, c. 1900. Built in 1887, on the occasion of Queen Victoria's Golden Jubilee, the well was then the only public water supply for the whole village, but, in line with Victorian thinking, it was locked to prevent its use on Sundays.

The Church, Seer Green.

Pictured in around 1920 from Chalfont Road, Holy Trinity Church had been built on the village green in 1846, using local flints with stone dressings. Before its construction, Seer Green had been a remote part of the Parish of Farnham Royal, and church attendance involved a round trip of some 15 miles.

High Street, Seer Green.

Turning to look along Chalfont Road, here given the grandiose title of High Street, the same photographer captures the other side of the road, and the old buildings which for generations had faced the green. The nearest cottages have closely woven hurdles as garden fences, and the pub next door is covered with creeper which has smothered all the frontage and almost hidden its projecting sign.

On this postcard from the thirties, the Jolly Cricketers with its creeper well under control, and the four cottages of Prospect Place, face the churchyard across Chalfont Road. At this date, guides for the increasing number of Chiltern ramblers recommended the teas served at both of Seer Green's public houses, one at each end of the churchyard.

Looking back along the same section of Chalfont Road in the early thirties, Wilkinson's newsagents and tobacconists shop, an offshoot from their main premises near Beaconsfield station, has been added on the corner with its distinctive angled frontage, next to Prospect Place.

Beaconsfield Road, Seer Green.

This 1920 view down Church Street beside the church includes the other pub, The Three Horseshoes. The children were either deliberately posed for the picture or had been following the photographer around the village, for this picture includes the same group who were by the roadside in the views of Chalfont Road from the same postcard series.

The General Post Office, Seer Green.

Looking from the corner of the churchyard, again around 1920, and with the same children yet again, this is the view into Chalfont Road as it leads out of the village centre The cottage on the right, which had been a private school in the previous century, was then 'The Bakery' which also housed the post office, before its move to Church Road.

127

CHALFONT ROAD, SEER GREEN.

Further out of the village along Chalfont Road, but looking back toward the centre, this picture was taken in the early thirties when, despite the first development on side turnings, there were still some cherry orchards beside the road, with well-trimmed boundary hedges.

Half a mile from the centre of Seer Green, Chalfont Road passes the old Ponds Farm, photographed in 1906. During the Second World War it was taken over by the army, and then became a hostel for homeless children. In 1955 it was bought by the Spastics Society and extended as a residential home for people with cerebral palsy, now known as 'the Princess Marina Centre.